the Perpetual Book Fund

A

Colonial Italian American Organization

Perpetual Book Fund Book

WILLIAMSBURG REGIONAL LIBRARY FOUNDATION

FARE LA CODA · SCARPE · NE · CAFFE · LA FAMIGLIA · AN MO · SUPERSTIZIONI · ITALIANISSIMO · LA GONDOLA · APERITIVO · PASSEGGIATA · ITALISSI · AN MO · CHIAROSCURO · ITALIANISSIMO · BODONI · AN MO · OCCHIALI · GIARDINI · GELATO · MANGIARE · AN MO · ITALIANISSIMO · ITALISSI · LA VESPA · LA DONNA · APERITIVO · PIZZA

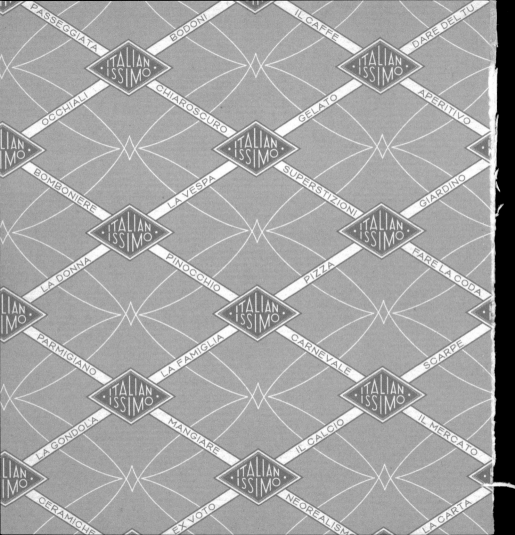

ITALIANISSIMO

. . . .

THE QUINTESSENTIAL GUIDE
TO WHAT ITALIANS
DO BEST

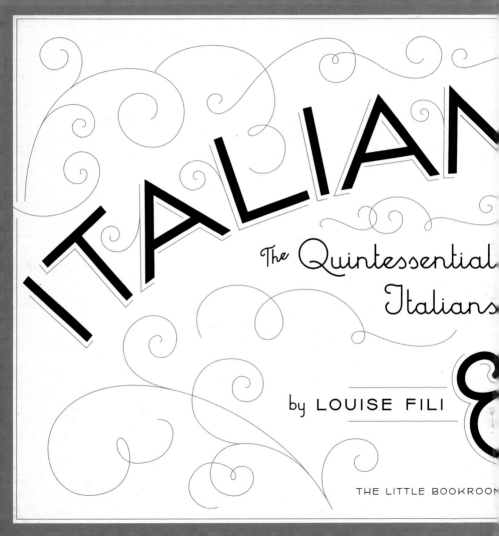

ITALIAN

The Quintessential
Italians

by LOUISE FILI

THE LITTLE BOOKROOM

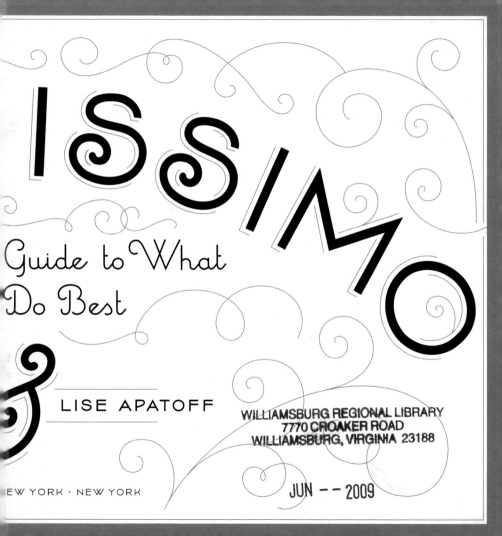

ISSIMO

Guide to What Do Best

LISE APATOFF

EW YORK · NEW YORK

TABLE of CONTENTS

....

L'INDICE

©2008 The Little Bookroom • Text ©2008 Louise Fili and Lise Apatoff

Design: Louise Fili and Jessica Hische, Louise Fili Ltd.

Printed in China • All rights reserved, which includes the right to reproduce this book or portions thereof in any form whatsoever.

Library of Congress Cataloging-in-Publication Data

Fili, Louise.

Italianissimo : the quintessential guide to what Italians do best / by Louise Fili and Lise Apatoff.

p. cm.

Includes bibliographical references.

ISBN 1-892145-54-5 (alk. paper)

1. Italy—Civilization. 2. Italy—Social life and customs. 3. Cookery, Italian. 4. Arts, Italian.
5. National characteristics, Italian. 6. Italy—Miscellanea. I. Apatoff, Lise. II. Title.

DG441.F55 2008

945—dc22

2008007966

Published by The Little Bookroom • 435 Hudson Street, 3rd floor • New York NY 10014

editorial@littlebookroom.com • www.littlebookroom.com

10 9 8 7 6 5 4 3 2 1

Distributed in the U.S. by Random House, in the U.K. and Ireland by Signature Book Services, and by Random House International.

Page 9: © Atlantide Phototravel/Corbis • *Page 12:* © Augusto Casasoli/A3/Contrasto • *Page 15:* Via Veneto, Rome, 1960. Luce Institute/Alinari Archive Management, Florence. • *Page 23:* Rivoire, Florence. Walter Vogel/Imagno/Getty Images/Getty Images • *Page 25:* Martin Rose/Getty Images • *Page 29:* Archivio Fotografico Fondazione Carnevale di Viareggio • *Page 36:* Credit line accompanies image. • *Page 40:* Advertisement for the Fiat 500, circa 1957. Touring Club Italiano/Alinari Archives Management, Milano. • *Page 44:* Sophia Loren, Rome, 1956. © ANSA/Corbis • *Page 48:* Courtesy of Marcia Lippman and Rosella Matt. *Page 50:* Echos/(re)view/Jupiterimages • *Page 54:* Gelateria, Rome. © PNC/Brand X/Corbis • *Page 57:* Illustrations by Renato Alarcao • *Page 58:* © Villa Gamberaia • *Page 61:* © Dan Brìški; iStockphoto.com/ Chamois • *Page 62:* Monticchiello, Tuscany. © Doug Pearson/JAI/Corbis • *Page 65:* Outdoor trattoria in Rome, 1927. Bruni Archive/Alinari Archives Management, Florence. • *Page 66:* Grateful son at the finish line, 1968 © RAI - su licenza Fratelli Alinari. • *Page 72:* Emilio Pucci and model on the terrace of the Pucci Building in Florence,1955. Fosco Maraini/Gabinetto Vieusseux Property©Fratelli Alinari. • *Page 75:* Movie still from *Ladri di Biciclette*, 1948. The Film Stills Archive of The Museum of Modern Art • *Page 76:* Eyeglasses, circa 1954. Courtesy of Lino di Nardo, Antica Occhialeria, Florence. • *Page 80:* Renata Tebaldi at the Teatro Manzoni in Milan, 1957. Toscani Archive/Alinari Archives Management, Florence. • *Page 87:* Massimo Borchi/Atlantide Phototravel • *Page 97:* Piazzaiolo, Naples. © Atlantide Phototravel/ Corbis • *Page 98:* Piazza del Popolo, Ascoli Piceno. © Atlantide Phototravel/Corbis • *Page 100:* Shoe lasts of the stars, Ferragamo, 1952. Toscani Archive/Alinari Archives Management, Florence. • *Page 105:* Illustrations by Jessica Hische. • *Page 109:* Grape harvest, 1946. Bruni Archive/Alinari Archives Management, Florence. • *Page 110:* Actress Lucia Bosé with husband Luis Miguel Dominguin driving a Vespa in Rome. Luce Institute/Alinari Archive Management, Florence. • All other images from the collection of Louise Fili.

A NOTE FROM THE AUTHORS

WITH THE MENTION OF THE WORD ITALY, A FLOOD OF SENSE MEMORIES ARE RELEASED: LIGHT-FILLED LANDSCAPES, VOLUPtuous markets, unforgettable meals, breathtaking art, expressive language, and generous strangers—even for those who have never set foot there. This is a seductive culture which inspires undeniable romanticism, and has captured the imaginations of many. Quite simply, everything tastes better, sounds better, and looks better in Italian.

This book is an affectionate and eclectic portrait of that which is essentially Italian, or *Italianissimo*—a celebration of the culture and quirks that continue to intrigue, endear, and inspire all devotees of Italy. *Buon Viaggio!*

We would like to thank our enthusiastic publisher, Angela Hederman, for encouraging us to write this book.

In Italy, mille grazie to Mariangela Catalani of Le Stanze di Santa Croce, where a good part of this book was written; Lino di Nardo of Antica Occhialeria; Valentina Roselli and Aniello Scognamiglio at the Mercato di Sant'Ambrogio; Laura Giuntini of Alinari; Carlo Saitta; Ilse Girona; and sisters-in-law Anna, Alba, and Gabriella.

In the United States, we are grateful to Rosella Matt, Wendy Wolf, Krystyna Skalski, Marcia Lippman, Nancy Haslam, and Jackie Roberts for their invaluable assistance. At Louise Fili Ltd, a very special thanks to Jessica Hische for her extraordinary design and Photoshop work, and to Andy Evans for his expertise.

And finally, our deepest thanks to our families, Steven and Nicolas Heller and Mario and Lorenzo Acciai for their continued love and support.

Louise Fili and Lise Apatoff

L'ACETO BALSAMICO

....

BALSAMIC VINEGAR

THE REGION OF EMILIA-ROMAGNA, PERCHED ABOVE THE APENNINE MOUNTAINS, HAS ALWAYS BEEN SYNONYMOUS with good food. Parmesan cheese, Parma hams, mortadella, tortellini, and lasagna are just some of its culinary stars. One of its most versatile and mysterious products is *aceto balsamico di Modena.* Although classified a vinegar, balsamic is actually produced in a very different process. The *mosto,* or grape must, is made from the seeds, pulp, and juice of fresh local grapes, which is simmered for hours until reduced by half. Then begins the long journey through a series of five barrels, each made from a different variety of wood, imparting its own distinctive flavor; with each passage, the vinegar is reduced again by half. It can take anywhere from twelve to fifty years to make the finished product—the sweet, dark, tangy syrup that is used drop by drop to enhance and exalt the flavor of everything from veal to strawberries.

....

Only that which is made in Modena is real *aceto balsamico.* Accept no substitutes, and make your way to the source: Giusti, on Via Farina 75, carries a signature line of the finest balsamic vinegars in varying degrees of age. A family business since 1605, this elegant shop with a Liberty-style facade is well worth the visit, as is their tiny *osteria* of only four tables—a short walk through a back hallway—which offers an unparalleled dining experience. The restaurant is open for lunch only. Reserve ahead. *Way* ahead. Tel/fax: 011 39 059 222 533

L'APERITIVO

....

I T IS NOT QUITE DINNERTIME, YET EXUBERANT CROWDS ARE SPILLING INTO THE STREETS WITH BRIGHTLY colored drinks in hand. What are they doing? Preparing for their next meal. *"Prendiamo un aperitivo."* (Let's have an aperitif.) The term itself is derived from *"che apre"*—that which opens (in this case, the stomach)—to successive libations, which is to say that it is a drink taken before meals to stimulate the appetite. The ancient Romans consumed *aperitivi* made from honey, wine, and spices. Subsequently, monastic orders concocted elixirs from hundreds of different herbs, essences, roots, flowers, and citrus, infused in alcohol and miraculous in their restorative powers.

As afternoon drifts into evening and shops close for the day, *caffè* bartenders start laying out an inviting array of little salted snacks, or *stuzzichini*—from *stuzzicare*, to poke (that appetite again!). Matrons in furs, workers in dusty overalls, elegantly suited lawyers, and young moderns in designer jeans all congregate to chatter animatedly in front of the *caffè* bar, reaching, snacking, joking, and sipping, as they unwind and make dinner plans. After all that stimulation, the appetite may become overexcited, but not to worry—after dinner, one can always order a *digestivo*.

LE AUTORITÀ

. . . .

THE UBIQUITOUS PRESENCE OF ITALY'S NUMEROUS LAW ENFORCERS, WHO SPORT STYLISH UNIFORMS, polished leather boots, and requisite automatic weapons, can be intimidating and confusing to the uninitiated. Instead of instilling a sense of trust, they can have the opposite effect —off-putting and at times perplexing—even for Italians, who prefer to avoid these guardians of justice whenever possible.

CARABINIERI

UNIFORM (variously attributed to Armani and Valentino): black with broad red stripe along pants; imposing tall hat with silver flame
WHERE: every *comune*, or township
DUTIES: law and order, and then some

POLIZIA MUNICIPALE

UNIFORM (formerly designed by Pucci): dark blue with light blue shirt; white helmet
WHERE: piazzas and roadblocks
DUTIES: traffic violations, road security, zoning infractions

POLIZIA DI STATO

UNIFORM: grey blue, with purple stripe and accents
WHERE: main city of every province
DUTIES: anyone's guess, but include passports, green cards, public security

GUARDIA DI FINANZA

UNIFORM: grey with yellow facing; flame on hat gives nickname *"Fiamme Gialle"*
WHERE: wherever you least expect
DUTIES: tax evasion, smuggling, fake Prada bags and sunglasses

LA BELLA FIGURA

L*A BELLA FIGURA*, LITERALLY BEAUTIFUL FIGURE, IS A CONCEPT NOT EASILY GRASPED OUTSIDE OF ITALY. The unspoken understanding that appearance and behavior are taken into consideration by the world at large is part of the basic fabric of Italian tradition. *"Cosa penserà la gente?"* (What will people think?) *Bella figura* is not only about looking good and using the right fork, but encompasses inherent dignity and the awareness that certain circumstances require certain behavior: the *alta società* enrobed in the fashion of the season, the housewife who makes sure that neighbors know that her floors are washed daily, the stone mason who goes for coffee with polished shoes and a pressed shirt, the farmer who gives his best food to the sheep shearers so that word of his generosity will spread. Public life historically took place in the piazzas, and therefore it was not unusual for two Italians to know each other for years without ever being invited to the other's home, making it possible to present oneself as desired. Because college tuition is free, most Italians have no need to put their money in the bank, preferring instead to spend it for their own immediate gratification—and for those who hopefully will be looking.

CAVOLONE
BIG CABBAGE

BELLISSIMO

THE BEST, THE FIRST, THE BIGGEST: EVERYTHING IS HEIGHTENED BY AN ITALIAN'S NATURAL PASSION for exalting the topic at hand. The significance of a word can take on new meaning simply by tacking on an ending: *bello* (beautiful) is elevated to *bellissimo* (very beautiful), *bellino* (beautiful, little and cute), *bellona* (a lovely, showy, unrefined woman), and *belloccia* (a large, florid, provocative, yet refined woman). There is nothing affected or theatrical in the use of superlatives in everyday speech; these terms are used by the youngest (*giovanissimi*) to the oldest (*vecchissimi*) and from the illiterate to the most learned. The simplest discussion of the day's events, or even where to have coffee, can become infinitely more colorful and interesting with just a little exaggeration.

PER ESEMPIO			
CASA	house	CASOTTO	shed
CASINA	small house	CASOTTINO	little shed
CASETTA	insignificant house	CASALE	farmhouse
CASONA	a big and slightly ugly house	CASAMENTO	tenement house
CASACCIA	a big and *really* ugly house	CASELLO	tollbooth
CASINO	bordello or big mess	CASELLA	P.O. box, pigeonhole
CASUPOLA	simple little cottage	CASATA	lineage

MA LA VOLP

col suo balzo,

raggiunto il quieto F

18 pt. Ma la volpe, col suo balzo,

16 pt. Ma la volpe, col suo balzo, ha

14 pt. Ma la volpe, col suo balzo, ha rag

12 pt. Ma la volpe, col suo balzo, ha raggiunto

10 pt. Ma la volpe, col suo balzo, ha raggiunto il

8 pt. Ma la volpe, col suo balzo, ha raggiunto il quieto Fido.

Ma la volpe, col suo balzo, h

Ma la volpe, col su

Ma la volpe, col su

Ma la volpe, col suo

Ma la volpe, col suo

BODONI

....

GIAMBATTISTA BODONI, AN ENGRAVER, PRINTER, AND TYPOGRAPHER, COMBINED THE AESTHETIC IDEALS OF classicism with the requisites of contemporary technology. The timeless result was a graceful typeface known for its bold strokes contrasted with fine hairlines—a formidable technical task in the eighteenth century. Arguably Italy's most emblematic typeface, Bodoni has certainly become one of the world's most commonly used letterforms. Although the font has been revived and redrawn by numerous type designers since its inception, it has always retained its elegance, especially in comparison to the monotone "old style" of its English predecessors. Bodoni's letterforms and his seminal treatise on typography, *Manuale Tipografico*, though centuries old, are still consulted by designers the world over, a testament to the durability of a type that has the transparent clarity of a crystal goblet and the style of an era.

....

Il Museo Bodoniano, located on the top floor of the stately Palazzo della Pilotta in Parma, is a must-see for the aficionado of typography or fine printing. While examining the heart-stopping *Manuale Tipografico* or any other of 1,000-and-counting volumes here, do not be surprised to find yourself being closely followed by a serious attendant with dustcloth in hand. Admission is free, though reservations are required; be sure to email or fax ahead. Strada alla Pilotta 3, Parma; Tel: 011 39 0521/220411 • Fax: 011 39 0521/235662; Email: mubodoni@unipr.it

LE BOMBONIERE

AN ITALIAN WEDDING, CHRISTENING, GRADUATION, OR FIRST COMMUNION WOULD BE UNTHINKABLE WITHOUT traditional *bomboniere,* a type of elaborate party favor. Sugar-covered almonds (*confetti*), signifying prosperity and fertility, have long been given to guests as an auspicious memento. Today, the token sweets are inserted into creative arrangements of colored ribbons, flowers, and tulle, combined with silver, porcelain, crystal, and ceramic figurines. A great deal of thought goes into selecting *bomboniere*; entire families will confer at length, while munching on numerous samples. Not a small investment, *confetti* come in an infinite choice of colors, sizes, and quality, and have even inspired a Museo del Confetto in Andria. The almonds of the Abruzzo region are the most prized, particularly those of Sulmona, birthplace of Ovid. Equally noteworthy are the elaborate baskets used to present the *bomboniere*, which can be masterpieces of engineering ingenuity; the oohs and aahs of admiration are often directed to the basket as well as the newborn.

The new socially conscious generation sometimes opts to give to charity rather than assume the indulgent cost of wedding favors. Nonetheless, tradition runs so deep that *bomboniere* shops continue to flourish all over Italy, in small towns as well as big cities.

IL CAFFÈ

·············

COFFEE

A BARISTA, LIKE A SYMPHONY MAESTRO, ORCHES-TRATES A LITANY OF REQUESTS IN RAPID SUCCESSION: *cappuccino, espresso, macchiato, corretto, lungo, doppio ristretto, bollente, tiepido, in vetro.* The hissing of the milk steamer, the thumping of filters being emptied, the clatter of the cups and saucers, the clinking of tiny spoons, and the enveloping heavenly aroma are a feast for all the senses. Spirited simultaneous conversations from the constant stream of loyal clientele cover subjects as broad as soccer scores, love affairs, daily headlines, politics, and the last or the next meal. Lingering is not the point here; espresso is meant to be consumed quickly, while standing at the bar. One can enjoy *un caffè* anytime, but cappuccino must never, *never* be ordered after a meal as it impedes the digestion, and will brand you as a foolhardy tourist.

AQUA VIRGO

After a young maiden led thirsty soldiers to refreshment at a clear spring in the hills beyond ancient Rome, the prized Aqua Virgo (virgin water) was harnessed and pumped through aqueducts to supply the newly erected Pantheon. This supports the claim that the best coffee in Rome—or Italy, or the world, for that matter—is to be found in the bars of this neighborhood, where the faucets still run with the same precious H_2O. One favorite haunt, Sant'Eustachio (Piazza di Sant'Eustachio 82), teems with regulars experiencing caffeine bliss, while other devotees swear by the nearby Tazza d'Oro (Via degli Orfani 84). Neither will disappoint.

IL CALCIO

ICK, KICK, KICK, KICK. IMPRINTED IN THE GENETIC PATTERNING OF THE YOUNG ITALIAN MALE IS THE automatic impulse to have an acrobatic and energetic dialogue with any spherical object—especially if it happens to be a soccer ball. Fans are staunchly loyal to two teams: first, to their regional *squadra* (such as Roma, Fiorentina, or Milan), where age-old competitiveness flares up with gusto at the games; and second, to the national team, the *Azzurri*, named for the blue color of the jerseys. The players are heroes—at least for the season—and top designers vie for the honor of fashioning the uniforms. Soccer has been called Italy's only form of patriotism, as regional differences are forgotten during the championship games—the one time that citizens from up and down the boot speak of themselves proudly as "Italians." When the soccer season comes around, no plans are made for Sundays after lunch; this is a time sacred to *tifosi* (fans—derived from the word *typhus*, describing their feverish behavior) to watch the game. The more passionate will head for the stadium, while others prefer to congregate in front of the television at the local *circolo* where they can watch, moan, cheer, gasp, and hoot in like company.

IL CAPODANNO

EVERY DECEMBER, RED UNDERWEAR BEGINS TO MAKE AN APPEARANCE IN SHOP WINDOWS OF *MERCERIE* throughout Italy, in anticipation of *Capodanno*, or New Year's. The color red is reputed to eschew the evil eye; the tighter it is worn to the body, the more effective its powers for bringing luck in the coming year.

Naples takes the custom a step further. The locals not only replace their underwear, but are also known to discard old dishes, appliances, and furniture literally right out the window. The purging is accompanied by homemade fireworks displays which some liken to a battleground—or perhaps an eruption of Mount Vesuvius. No *napoletano* would dream of daring to walk the streets in the early hours of the first day of January.

Housecleaning notwithstanding, it is the meal, or *cenone*, that is the focus of New Year's Eve. Lentils, often paired with pig's trotter, or *zampone*, are always present on the menu, traditionally symbolizing good fortune in the new year. After a hearty repast, dancing, or *tombola* (bingo) follows well into the night.

Until 1582, the new year was celebrated on March 25th (the Annunciation), the day archangel Gabriel announced to the Virgin that she had been chosen for a miraculous birth.

IL CARNEVALE

. . . .

L ITERALLY "GOODBYE TO THE FLESH," *CARNEVALE* IS A LAST CHANCE TO EAT MEAT, AND ENJOY LIFE'S OTHER excesses, before the forty-day sentence of Lent is served. *A carnevale ogni scherzo vale*: At *carnevale*, anything goes. Traditionally a period when roles were reversed—commoners trading places with nobility, men dressed as women and vice-versa—this is a time for parades, outrageous costumes, lively music, masquerade balls, and streets peppered with multicolored confetti. Though abolished by Mussolini, *carnevale* returned with a vengeance in 1979 to Venice, where it is held during the ten days leading up to *Martedì Grasso* (Fat Tuesday). Viareggio devotes a staggering five weekends to the festivities, where elaborate floats of papier-mâché caricatures lampooning public figures are an annual barometer of the ever-turbulent political scene.

LA BATTAGLIA DELLE ARANCE

One of the most memorable carnevale celebrations can be found in the lovely town of Ivrea, in the Piedmont region. A traditional three-day battle in which sizeable teams of fighters and horse-drawn carts lob tens of thousands of oranges at one another (with no face or body protection) results in a sweetly-citrus-scented city bathed in the juice of Sicilian blood oranges, which are sent up north by train every year for the event. The sixty tons of oranges are for the sole purpose of weaponry, and are never eaten, though polenta and cod are shared post-battle.

LA CARTA

....

PARER

SCRAPING GOATSKINS TO MAKE SHEETS FOR DOCUMENTS, ILLUMINATED MANUSCRIPTS, AND OTHER PURPOSES WAS a costly and time-consuming procedure—therefore paper was a greatly heralded invention. The Arabs learned the craft from their Chinese prisoners following an eighth-century war; by the twelfth century it had made its way to the Maritime Republic of Amalfi, where artisans quickly excelled at their craft, making this exquisite rag paper the material of choice for papal and official documents. Within a century the central eastern town of Fabriano began manufacturing paper, and by the 1400s was exporting a million sheets a year to Florence and Venice, both major book producers. The Florentines decorated their endpapers by dipping sheets into large vats of brilliant colors to create marbled effects, basket-weave patterns, and swirling designs inspired by *pavone*, or peacock tails. The *filigrana*, or watermark, made from original copper molds, was invented at Fabriano, whose name is still synonymous with fine papermaking today.

....

Il Museo della Carta e della Filigrana in Fabriano (located in the un-touristy Ancona province, in the region of le Marche) features exhibits and workshops in papermaking and watermarking, making this a destination for the paper enthusiast. www.museodellacarta.com/ing/

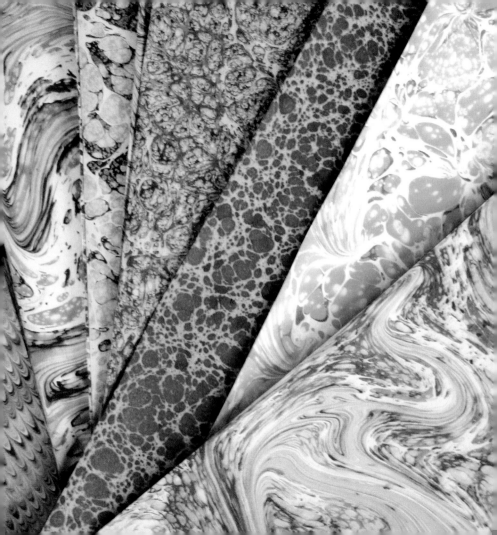

LA CARTA D'ARANCIA

THE ORANGE WRAPPER

O NCE A PRACTICAL MEASURE USED TO PROTECT FRUIT FROM DAMAGE OR DISEASE IN TRANSIT, THE ORANGE wrapper is still in use today, if for no other purpose than pure visual delight. Making its star turn in Italian open-air markets, where the *agrumi* (citrus) are piled high into seductive pyramids, only a precious strategically placed few come with the prize of a colorful wrapper, twisted around the fruit and begging to be taken home.

Subjects run the gamut from virile men, sexy women, and adorable children, to circus performers, giraffes, birds, flowers, and mythical creatures. Designed and printed in Sicily, these are some of the best examples of contemporary commercial folk art.

PROCURING A WRAPPED ORANGE

Buying an orange in the market with its wrapper intact is a delicate negotiation, since the one you want will most likely be the lynchpin of the whole mound of carefully arranged fruit. Sincerity (with a dash of hyperbole) is recommended; tell the vendor that you want that particular specimen because the wrapper is so extraordinarily beautiful, and you are a collector: *Scusi, Signore(a), ne volevo una con la carta perché è così bella e perché io sono collezionista.*

It is helpful to state this early on, since sometimes the seller will brusquely tear off the wrapper to make sure that the orange is good! Of course, it would make everyone happier in this transaction if you were to purchase a *mezzo chilo* (half a kilo; a little over a pound), or more precisely, *cinque etti* (1 *etto*=3.5 ounces).

LE CERAMICHE

ITALIAN CERAMICS

OR CENTURIES, POPES AND KINGS DINED ON GLEAM-
ING SILVER OR ENAMELED PLATES, WHILE PEASANTS
ate from roughly hewn wood or clay. The humble vessel was
changed forever when Arabic techniques for brilliant color and
double-glazing migrated to Italy. By the mid-1400s there were
many different centers of Italian Majolica production, each with
its own distinctive style, many of which are still prevalent today.
Vietri, on the Amalfi coast, uses bright colors and bold patterns
to decorate every surface: tableware, chandeliers, elegant palazzo
floors and balconies, as well as colorful church roofs. Deruta, in
Umbria, is best known for incorporating Raphael's intricate images
of golden-hued mythological creatures. In Tuscany, Montelupo
artisans create overall patterns favoring birds in distinctive shades
of deep blue. Planters produced in Caltagirone, Sicily, depict the
heads of legendary knights and moors who gaze disconcertingly
from terraces throughout the island. In the fifteenth century, Luca
della Robbia brought the craft to a higher yet affordable art form
with his signature cerulean and white ceramics. These distinctive
garlanded plaques portraying Madonnas and cherubs still adorn
parish churches and tabernacles all over the Italian countryside.

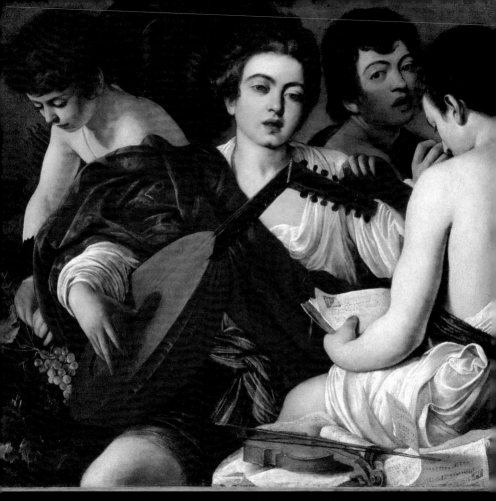

Caravaggio (Michelangelo Merisi da) (1573-1610). The Musicians. Ca 1595. Oil on canvas, 36 ¼ x 46 ⅝ in (92.1 x 118.4 cm). Rogers Fund, 1952 (52.81).
The Metropolitan Museum of Art, New York, NY, U.S.A. Image © The Metropolitan Museum of Art/Art Resource, NY.

IL CHIAROSCURO

....

BY THE LATE RENAISSANCE, PAINTERS HAD THOROUGHLY EXPLORED THE REALMS OF NATURALISM, REALISM, PER-spective, and beauty. Leonardo da Vinci was one of the first to model his figures with dark and light underpainting rather than line. In the late sixteenth century, however, the painter Caravaggio defied convention, astounding his viewers with the unusual drama of sharply lit figures emerging from the dark. His paintings, full of emotion and movement, caught the moment like photographs, using stark contrast to emphasize the realism. Immediately, other artists began incorporating his innovative use of light onto canvas, first in Italy and eventually throughout Europe, creating a visual commentary on the social and political unrest of the times. *Chiaroscuro* (literally *light dark*) allowed painters the ability to depict life illuminated by candlelight in an innovative, realistic manner. Daily events became commonplace in art: boisterous tavern scenes, commoners playing cards, doctors in operating theatres, and young lovers deep in conversation. Traditional biblical subject matter—swooping angels, nocturnal Madonnas, and saints in various states of anguish and ecstasy—were now memorably depicted in this tenebrous style.

ORARIO DI LAV

(Art. 12 del R.D.L. 15 Marzo 1923, n. 692)

chiuso la

domenica

ENTRATA	RIPOSO	US
ALLE ORE 9,00	DALLE ORE 12,30 ALLE ORE 13,30	ALLE

SABATO: 9,00 - 13,30

ANDO L'ORARIO NON E' COMUNE PER TUTTO IL PERSONALE LE INDICAZIONI SOPRASEGNATE
ORTATE PER REPARTO O CATEGORIA PROFESSIONALE O PERSONALE. QUANDO IL LAVO
SQUADRE, DOVRANNO ESSERE RIPORTATE LE INDICAZIONI SUACCENNATE PER CIASCUNA

(REGOLAMENTO del D.L. 15-3-1923 n. 692)

TTA ....

LLA OBBLIGATORIA ESENTE DA BOLLO

6   6

ERTURA   POMERIGGIO   CHIUSURA

CHIUS
SI APRE ALLE O

12   3   9   3

CHIUSO

. . . .

CLOSED

F OR VISITORS TO ITALY, THE CRUELEST WORD OF ALL IS *CHIUSO* (KEE-U'-SO), OR CLOSED. POSTED IN a shop or museum window, it is often paired with *per restauri* (for restoration), *per sciopero* (on strike), or *per lutto* (in mourning). All shops have a *chiusura settimanale* (a half-day closing per week, which varies from city to city). A holiday falling close to a weekend gives a shopkeeper an ideal excuse to make a *ponte* (bridge) and close his doors to head to the seaside for a long weekend. Slightly more nebulous albeit hopeful is the hastily written *torno subito* (be right back). Did the *proprietario* go for a quick coffee, an assignation, or...? Don't despair. Find something else to do. You'll soon forget your original destination and discover something equally intriguing.

Twice a year, on the first of May and the fifteenth of August, the entire country comes to a virtual halt, as signs announce *chiuso per festa*. On *Primo Maggio* (Italy's Labor Day), no buses are in operation, and newspapers are not published the following day. *Ferragosto* (the Assumption of the Madonna) often marks the midpoint of summer holidays, with the traditional mass exodus and choking traffic jams that ensue.

LA CINQUECENTO

WHAT IS THE SUBJECT OF A LOVE SONG, A CHARACTER IN AN ANIMATED FILM, AND HAS DOORS THAT make men weep? The Fiat 500, of course. In the 1930s while England had the Morris 8 and Germany the Volkswagen, Mussolini's Italy experienced vehicle envy. To address the problem, Fiat chairman Giovanni Agnelli summoned his engineers to create a car for the masses. After the head designer came up with a model that caught fire on its test run (with Agnelli in tow), he was summarily dismissed, and Dante Giacosa came on board. His solution, the 500, was introduced with great fanfare in 1936, and dubbed Topolino (Mickey Mouse) for its disarming cuteness. An overnight sensation, it was able to conquer winding medieval roads as well as hopeless parking situations. The rear-engined Nuova Fiat 500, or Cinquecento, followed in 1957, featuring reverse-opening "suicide doors" which were later discontinued—much to the disappointment of many an Italian male who could no longer gawk at the shapely legs of a *signora* entering and exiting the car. Although production ceased in 1975, making it a coveted collector's item, the Cinquecento made a triumphant reappearance in 2007, on the fiftieth anniversary of its auspicious debut.

DARE DEL TU

. . . .

THE TU FORM

WHILE THE ENGLISH LANGUAGE MAY HAVE ONLY ONE WORD FOR *YOU*, IN ITALIAN THERE ARE three: *tu* (familiar), *Lei* (polite) and *voi* (plural). *Tu* is used without question when addressing children, family, close friends, and lovers. Upon meeting a business associate, official, or elder for the first time, one must use *Lei* until instructed otherwise. You will be asked: *Potremmo darci del tu?* (Can we use the *tu* form?). It is considered impolite to assume informality unless agreed upon. One never stops using *Lei* with police, professors, and priests, and some women will spend the better part of their married lives addressing their mothers-in-law without ever daring to *dare del tu*.

TU VS. LEI

In 1939 the Fascist party abolished the Lei form, calling it a "witness…to the centuries of serfdom and abjection." Instead, they embraced the *tu* form, which expressed the "universal value of Rome and Christianity," and the *voi* form "as a sign of respect and of hierarchical recognition." A women's magazine of the time with the misfortune to be called *Lei* (which also means "she" in Italian) was forced to change its name to *Annabella*.

During the anti-Mafia trials in Sicily in the late 1980s, tireless prosecutor Giovanni Falcone succeeded in eliciting testimonies from many Mafiosi due in part to his use of the *Lei* form, which was taken as a term of respect, while other magistrates patronized the defendants by addressing them with the belittling *tu*.

LA DONNA ITALIANA

....

HE TWO MOST CITED FEMALES IN THE ITALIAN LANGUAGE ARE *LA MAMMA* AND *LA MADONNA*, BOTH of whom are invoked in moments of joy, fear, and rage: *"Mamma mia!" "O Madonna mia!"* While the traditional wedding toast may be *"Felicità e figli maschi"* (Happiness and male offspring), it is the woman—as confessor, disciplinarian, and procurer of favors, jobs, and pardons—around whom the family revolves.

CATERINA DE' MEDICI	1519–1589	Queen of France; brought ballet, the corset, fork, and tomato to the French
ARTEMESIA GENTILESCHI	1593–1653	Painter; won a lawsuit against her male teacher for sexual abuse
ELEONORA DUSE	1858–1924	Actress; first woman to be featured on the cover of *Time*
MARIA MONTESSORI	1870–1952	Educator; shown on the 1000 lire bill
ANNA MAGNANI	1908–1973	Actress; memorable role in *Open City*; won an Oscar for *The Rose Tattoo*
GAE AULENTI	1927–	Architect; designed the Musée d'Orsay in Paris
ORIANA FALLACI	1930–2006	Journalist and interviewer; humiliated Henry Kissinger

EX VOTO

....

THROUGH THE MIDDLE OF THE TWENTIETH CENTURY, EMBOSSED, CUT-OUT SILVER FIGURES, OR EX VOTOS, covered the interior walls of Italian churches, particularly in the south, bearing witness to the initiation of a vow, or *voto*. Whether the supplicant was seeking relief from a headache, heart disease, or sore feet, every body part was available for purchase, to be hung next to a favorite holy statue in hope of a cure. In addition, those relieved of an ailment would show their appreciation by bringing to the church proof of their devotion in the form of another ex voto stamped with either PGR—*per grazia ricevuta* (for grace received) or VFG—*voto fatto grazie* (vow granted, thank you).

Santa Lucia, whose eyes were gouged out because her Christian faith defied the Pagan times, is the go-to saint for anyone with vision problems. In her chapel in Siracusa, the profusion of medallions hanging on the walls is a testament to her efficacy.

Today, ex votos show up in jewelry stores, religious object shops, and flea markets, where they often look almost too shiny to pass for antique—though some vendors claim that it is a simple matter of "*molto olio di gomito*" (plenty of elbow grease).

BELLUNO

LA FAMIGLIA

....

NO ITALIAN WHO HAS A FAMILY IS EVER ALONE, WROTE LUIGI BARZINI, SUGGESTING THAT THE FAMILY IS THE only fundamental institution in the country. While Italy has suffered invasions, wars, occupations, and fleeting governments throughout history, the family has persevered.

In a country that is only slightly larger than the state of Arizona, it is difficult to get very far away from one's family. However, proximity is not viewed as a burden but an advantage. Freshly washed and ironed laundry, a place at the table for a home-cooked meal, *nonni*, or grandparents, who are always on call to babysit, and the vast network of relatives and friends comprise a support system that can help at any phase of life.

Need a job? An electrician? Help with that traffic ticket? A used car? A prospective wife? The answer is probably only a relation away. Most first homes are financed with family loans—no formal note, no interest. In the event of an emergency, *parenti*, or relatives, are the first to offer unconditional assistance.

Traditionally, the Italian woman retains her maiden name after marriage. This a not a feminist statement, but rather a reiteration of the familial tie. Family is forever.

FARE LA CODA

....

FOR ITALIANS, THE CONCEPT OF FORMING A LINE IS TEDIOUS AND BORING; THE ETIQUETTE OF WAITING HAS no place in their lives. In other cultures, a queue is a straight, ordered system, but *coda* (literally, "tail") runs counter to the Mediterranean sense of *libertà*. More like a football huddle, the Italian line is a product of not only a natural desire to be first, but a curiosity about other people's business. The fact is, if one has to wait, it might as well be entertaining—or at least informative. (A trip to the *farmacia* in search of a cure for a mother's swollen legs will undoubtedly result in personal advice from those waiting.) Because lines as we know them are nonexistent in Italy, when walking into a crowded shop one is obliged to call into the throng, *"Chi è l'ultimo?"* (Who is the last?) Nevertheless, beware of the slow, subtle weave forward—a well-practiced perpetrator will convince even *himself* that he was there before you. Of late, some modern-minded shopkeepers have taken the bold step to install take-a-number machines—to the consternation of many. After all, jiggling into a line can be an excuse for a conversation, a commentary, or just to let off steam— all infinitely more rewarding than simply waiting one's turn.

IL FIGLIO ITALIANO

. . . .

PREGNANCY ELEVATES A WOMAN TO A NEW STATUS IN THE ITALIAN COMMUNITY, AND THE BIRTH OF A CHILD is an auspicious event with miraculous overtones, heralded by the placement of a large bow of pale pink or blue satin on the front door. The new *bambino* is duly cuddled, coddled, passed from hand to hand, overdressed, overfed, and overindulged. Parental love is demonstrated by dressing one's offspring as elegantly as oneself, as is evidenced by the proliferation of exquisite clothing shops for children throughout Italy.

Naturalmente, an emphasis on nourishment begins early on: mothers weigh their infants after each nursing to insure that they are eating enough. And while parents may be indifferent to what goes on in the classroom, they come out in droves to critique the school cafeteria offerings. Early bedtimes? Not with 8 pm suppers. *Bambini* are pampered in every way: none, or very few, have obligations to the household; daily chores, even bed making, are taken care of by parents and grandparents. Children will live at home, *serviti e riveriti* (served and revered) through college and until they marry, when somehow, miraculously, they manage to grow up—to indulge children of their own.

Ripiegare all'indietro il piede della figura ed
incollarvi il paesaggio sottostante.
Seguendo la linea punteggiata, piegare in modo
da ottenere lo sfondo.

IL GELATO

. . . .

NOT JUST ICE CREAM

CLOSE YOUR EYES AND REVEL IN THE MOMENT. *DELIZIOSO.* IT ONLY TAKES A SPOONFUL OF GELATO TO INSURE reverie. More than a thousand years ago, the Arabs introduced sugar to Sicily along with a penchant for all things sweet. Who would have imagined that mixing the snows of Mount Etna with sugar and the sublime local, flavors—lemons, *mandarini*, blood oranges, citron, almonds, pistachios, and hazelnuts, as well as the incomparable essences of jasmine and roses—would deliver such enchantment?

True gelato is everything ice cream should be (and everything its American counterpart is not): less air, sugar, and butterfat, and more intensity of flavor. The serious *gelataio* uses only seasonal fruits and the freshest ingredients. The aficionado knows to seek out signs for *gelato artigianale* and tubs of stainless steel as opposed to plastic. Lurid colors and gaudy splashes of flavored syrups atop towering unmeltable mounds are to be avoided at all costs.

. . . .

It is no wonder that the finest artisanal gelato is still found in Sicily. In the baroque town of Noto, Corrado Costanzo makes magic with the delicate flavors of rose, jasmine, and *mandarino*. Via Silvio Spaventa 7/9, Noto, Sicily. Third-generation *gelataio* Antonio Lisciandro came north from Messina as a gelato "missionary" to open Carabé in Florence. His pistachio ice cream and almond granita have converted many. Via Ricasoli 60r, Florence.

I GESTI ITALIANI

. . . .

HAND GESTURES

LUIGI TRUNDLES DOWN THE STREET CARRYING AN OVERSIZED WATERMELON. WHEN ASKED THE TIME, HE carefully sets the watermelon down, and then wordlessly shrugs his shoulders while throwing up his hands, signifying "I don't know." One gesture is worth a thousand words, and talking hands are an integral part of Italian vocabulary and communication. People on the street seem to talk to themselves and gesticulate as though bewitched; they are on cell phones, or *telefonini*, earnestly trying to make themselves understood while hampered by the use of words only. A father can give his son an emphatic "No!" to his request to use the car by tapping his front tooth with his index finger. The son will implore by pressing his palms together at chest level, rocking them back and forth, while the exasperated mother cuts the air with two fingers in a scissors motion to tell them to cease—all in a crystal clear, silent exchange.

IT STARTED IN NAPLES

A densely populated, noisy city where life was lived in the street, Naples was instrumental in introducing hand gestures as a means of communication for all Italians. From upper stories of buildings, housewives would negotiate with vendors using sign language, then lower a basket with a rope for their wares. Residents from facing windows or balconies could easily converse above the din. And despite the very public aspect of Neapolitan life, a private conversation could be had in the crowded street through a mere exchange of glances.

IL GIARDINO ALL'ITALIANA

THE FIFTEENTH CENTURY WAS AN INSPIRED TIME WHEN FORTIFIED TOWERS WERE TRANSFORMED into country villas with loggias, where the elite could entertain lavishly. Architects and engineers competed to create beautiful, thought-provoking pleasure gardens with terraced layouts, sculptures, grottos, and ingenious water games to complement the magnificent frescoed villas. The Villa Lante outside of Viterbo was created as a summer residence where bishops, cardinals, and popes could gambol and hunt. A long stone table in the garden featured a fresh water canal on top for keeping wine and fruit cool, and one underneath for their holy toes. Imaginative use of boxwood, cypress, laurel, holly, and rosemary insured a consistently verdant garden throughout the seasons. Shaped and manicured, the shrubs were coaxed into swirling symmetric patterns which delineated spaces and created green labyrinths. Unusual botanical specimens were imported, including dwarf fruit trees, jasmine, and varieties of orange and lemon trees. Planted in grand terra-cotta pots and strategically placed in courtyards and borders, the citrus, which remained green year round, gave flowers and perfume in the summer and golden fruit in the winter.

LA GONDOLA

. . . .

BLACK BEAUTY

NO ONE TAKES A GONDOLA FOR ITS EFFICIENCY, BUT FOR ITS INDISPUTABLE ROMANCE. SADLY, ONLY A few hundred specimens remain afloat today in the canals of Venice. The gondola's graceful, dramatic silhouette, as well as its *ferro*, the curved comb-like piece of flat metal that adorns the prow, are universally recognized. Serving as a counterbalance to the heft of the gondolier, the *ferro* also denotes the six neighborhoods of Venice, while the single tooth on the opposite side represents the island of the Giudecca. Two hundred and eighty separate pieces, made from seven different types of wood, and five hundred hours of labor, go into the making of every gondola. Each should last fifty years, assuming the same owner, or someone of similar size, uses it. (Every gondola is custom-made according to the weight of the gondolier, and no two are alike.) By law, only the Venetian-born are allowed to practice the craft. Now appealing mostly to starry-eyed honeymooners and eager tourists, the gondola ride, though exorbitant, is still worth the indulgence. Nothing can better transmit the enchantment of Venice than to glide silently down the otherwise-inaccessible picturesque canals, far from the teeming crowds (but tell the singer to stay ashore).

LA LUCE

ITALIAN LIGHT

KNOWST THOU THE LAND WHERE THE LEMON TREES BLOOM, / WHERE THE GOLD ORANGE GLOWS IN THE DEEP THICKET'S GLOOM / WHERE A WIND EVER SOFT FROM THE BLUE HEAVEN BLOWS, / AND THE GROVES ARE OF LAUREL, AND MYRTLE AND ROSE? So wrote Goethe after his grand tour of Italy. How many artists and writers have been inspired to describe the autumn light playing over grapevines and dark-fingered cypress in Tuscany, the glittering rose glow over the Grand Canal in Venice, the endless blue horizons of the Amalfi coast, the gleaming white marble columns in Rome, the warm pink Umbrian hill towns, or the brilliant green wheat fields in a Sicilian spring? Italy celebrates an endless vocabulary of light on landscapes that change from morning to evening, north to south, season to season. The luminous vistas recorded by Leonardo da Vinci in his paintings can still be seen while traveling on any Tuscan road. Edith Wharton, E.M. Forster, and D.H. Lawrence all waxed poetic about their adoptive country. And filmmakers have eloquently translated Italian light on screen, from Bernardo Bertolucci's color-drenched interpretations to Vittorio De Sica's black-and-white cinematic ode to light, the poignant *Miracle in Milan*.

IL MANGIARE

....

WHERE ELSE IS A MEAL REMEMBERED WITH THE SAME TENDERNESS AND PASSION USUALLY RESERVED for a lover? Where else is the subject of dinner (past, present, or future) discussed at the breakfast table? Where else are food terms used to refer to character traits and body parts?

In Italy, of course. That said, an essential thing to understand about Italian cuisine is that it really doesn't exist. The cooking of Italy is distinguished by its regions, each with unique cultural influences, climates, and local ingredients. The Italians recognize the distinctive differences in the cooking of Naples or Venice or Lucca, which vary according to the fresh and flavorful seasonal produce available in these areas. While not every Italian may be brilliant in the kitchen, everyone is an authority on eating. No one would ever expect to find ripe crimson tomatoes in January or tender artichokes in July, nor deign to eat a flavorless greenhouse-grown variety out of season.

In order to enjoy a full gastronomic life, the Italians are intimate with and eager to talk about the workings of their digestive systems (*Come va l'intestino?*), avoiding cold drafts on the stomach, and paying obsessive attention to the *fegato*, or liver.

IL MASCHIO

ALTHOUGH THE BOTTOM-PINCHING, WOLF-WHISTLING STEREOTYPE IS LONG OUTDATED, THE ESSENCE OF the Latin Lover is intact. A soft voice, charming accent, and sleepy gaze would catch anyone's attention, but coupled with an earnest appreciation for women—while making them feel loved and desired—makes the Italian male irresistible. He has no qualms about weeping when something moves him, dressing with color and flair, buffing his nails, and embracing everyone. "Latin Lover" does not translate—Italians use the English term—however, men do not perceive themselves in this way. Actor Marcello Mastroianni actually felt obliged to accept roles against type in an effort to shed this label. Whether genetic or acquired, enduring or ephemeral, the art of *amore all'italiana* is undeniably seductive and endearing.

IL MAMMONE

The ubiquitous mammone—a big Mamma's boy—is a grown man living at home and shamelessly coddled by his adoring mother. The world naturally revolves around him and his every need; he remains a bachelor under the auspices of caring for his mother, but in fact it is because no wife could ever be so accommodating. This cultural phenomenon is vividly illustrated in Fellini's 1953 film classic, *I Vitelloni*, a portrait of five young men from a small town on the Adriatic who aimlessly while away their days in indulgent pleasures, to semi-tragic ends.

IL MERCATO

....

A N ITALIAN MARKET IS A STIMULATION OF ALL OF THE SENSES: VOLUPTUOUS PYRAMIDS OF GLEAMING violet eggplants, the taste of sun still lingering on vine-ripened tomatoes, the tender fuzz on blushing peaches, the heady bouquets of fresh-picked basil. An encyclopedia of varieties is offered by merchants loudly singing out their wares: *"Le vere ciliege di Vignola! Dolce come lo zucchero!"* (The real cherries of Vignola! Sweet as sugar!) *"Qua, qua! Il pesce salta ancora!"* (Here, here! The fish are still jumping!) *"Assaggia! Assaggia!"* (Taste it!) Circulating waiters from the market *caffè* pick up empty espresso cups and wine glasses and take orders for the next round. Rain or shine, steaming or freezing, the market prevails. While urban dwellers can choose from one or more daily markets, small towns will set aside one morning per week for the traveling vendors to put up stands in the center of town, with a range of offerings as broad as suckling pigs to women's corsetry.

Any questions about what to make for dinner, how to cook it, or the quantity necessary? The seller will be more than happy to offer an opinion, as will the nudging crowd proffering bags to be weighed and always ready to talk about the next meal.

LA MEZZALUNA

....

THE DICER

THE *MEZZALUNA* (HALF-MOON) OR MORE AFFECTION-ATELY, *LUNETTA*, OR MOONLET, IS THE KITCHEN UTENSIL of choice for all Italian cooks. The elegantly curved stainless steel blade attached to bulbous wooden handles is a staple in every household, and is as practical as it is beautiful. With one knob held in each hand, the cook makes a rhythmical rocking-back-and-forth motion to ensure equal pressure and a uniform dice. The mezzaluna is far safer than its French sibling, the chef's knife; it is almost impossible to cut yourself using it. Though often puzzling to the uninitiated, the mezzaluna will, after only a few attempts, turn the novice into a blade-wielding pro.

A well-seasoned mezzaluna in time leaves its own hollowed-out imprint in the wooden cutting board, forming a well for the next parsley and garlic to be chopped. Food processor? Housewives scoff at the homogeneous cut and the nuisance of washing its many components. The machine (undoubtedly a gift) will remain on the shelf as they reach for the utensil that got top billing in *La scienza in cucina e l'Arte di mangiare bene* (*The Science of Cookery and The Art of Eating Well*) by Pellegrino Artusi, the 1891 classic which still graces most kitchen shelves today.

LA MODA

....

FROM ROMAN TOGAS TO VELVET RENAISSANCE GOWNS, FROM CAPRI PANTS TO SLEEK CONTEMPORARY SUITS, Italians have always dressed with effortless elegance. Although blessed with an innate sense of style and a history of producing sumptuous textiles, it wasn't until 1952 that a struggling postwar Italy stunned the fashion world with its first formal international showing at the Sala Bianca in Florence's Palazzo Pitti. *La Moda Italiana* was born and embraced by a new generation looking for comfort and style. The success of the Italian fashion industry is unique due to strong family traditions and pride in craftsmanship: Gucci, Versace, Ferragamo, Fendi, Missoni, and Zegna are all multi-generational enterprises. The aristocratic Pucci family had been trading in silk for hundreds of years when young Emilio *(pictured at left)* wandered into fashion design almost by accident. Taking inspiration from the colorful flags of the Palio in Siena, he created signature prints of bright colors and kaleidoscopic geometric shapes on silk jersey that liberated the female figure. Pucci went so far as to prohibit his models from wearing girdles or stockings, a sensuous and revolutionary concept soon adopted by the fashion industry.

IL NEOREALISMO

....

NEOREALIST CINEMA

THE TRIALS AND TRIBULATIONS OF COMMON PEOPLE—
THEIR LOVE STORIES, WORK STRUGGLES, FAMILY
secrets and small town gossip—are all at the heart of the
films that Italians prefer over Hollywood extravaganzas. In the late
1940s a new crop of directors astounded audiences with movies
that poignantly mirrored the collective broken heart of a postwar nation. The cinematic studios, like the rest of Rome, were
in ruin, and money, film, and equipment were scarce. Shot on
location in black-and-white, using handheld cameras, this new
genre achieved a dramatic painterly effect in its genuine desire
to see people for what they were; there was no point in depicting
a romantic world no one could live in. Nonprofessional actors
were preferred for their authentic portrayals of a gritty realism
that captured the heroism of the ordinary citizen. When David
O. Selznick offered to finance Vittorio De Sica's *The Bicycle
Thief*—on the condition that Cary Grant be cast in the leading
role—De Sica would have nothing of it. Rather, this brilliant film
featured two unknowns in the role of father and son. The legacy
of Neorealist directors—De Sica, Roberto Rosellini, Lucchino
Visconti—continues to influence generations of filmmakers.

Il Museo Nazionale del Cinema houses five floors of movie memorabilia—thousands of films, books, scripts, posters, props, and costumes—in this landmarked dome in Turin. View continuously playing films in the generously proportioned main room while reclining on stylish red lounge chairs with built-in speakers. (Or flop down on the big round velvet bed and watch love scenes projected on the ceiling.) Via Montebello 20, Turin; www.museonazionaledelcinema.org

GLI OCCHIALI

. . . .

FOR THE REST OF THE WORLD, EYEGLASSES ARE WORN TO CORRECT VISION, BUT IN ITALY THEY ARE ABOVE all else a fashion statement. Armani, Gucci, Prada, and others design signature eyewear with their seasonal collections for adoring customers who change their *occhiali* with the same frequency, spending exorbitant sums for these highly visible status symbols. Sunglasses are an essential element of the Italian wardrobe from adolescence on, and are worn indoors and out, day and night, over the eyes, as a chic hairband, or as an elegant accessory when tucked into the neckline of a designer t-shirt. As with pasta, some experts credit the Chinese with the invention of eyeglasses. However, the existence of *occhiali* has been documented in both Pisa and Venice as early as 1285, both by historians and painters. Artist Tommaso da Modena depicted a bespectacled cardinal reading in 1352, and a dignified pair can be found hanging near Jerome's desk in Ghirlandaio's 1480 portrait of the saint. Florentines staunchly claim local hero Salvino d'Armato degli Armati as the inventor of the first wearable pair. Whatever the lineage, all agree that the most stylish specimens are to be found in Italy, *senza dubbio*.

L'OLIO D'OLIVA

....

OLIVE OIL

OLIO NUOVO, VINO VECCHIO (NEW OIL, OLD WINE) IS THE RULE FOR MANY ITALIAN CONNOISSEURS AND COOKS. All over the Mediterranean, olive oil has always been the foundation of cooking, as well as a cure-all for scores of minor ailments, including dry hair and chapped baby bottoms.

It can be daunting to choose from a shelf of olive oil in the store—peering at the colors and decoding the terminology—yet it is agreed that the brilliant green extra-virgin cold-pressed is the best: the younger, the better. Every oil-producing area in Italy has different varietals and methods of cultivation which subtly affect the flavor; Liguria's light golden oil is sweet and delicate, while that of Puglia and Sicily, which accounts for the majority of national production, has a heavier, riper flavor. Although each region proudly claims its local oil to be the best, the Tuscans are most vociferous. The smaller trees are more easily picked by hand, and the harvest takes place when the fruit is still partially unripe, which imparts its distinctive peppery flavor. The reputation of this oil is such that a Tuscan name on a label is a guaranteed marketing success. No matter what the region, a spoonful of *olio crudo,* drizzled just before serving, can enhance the flavor of the simplest of dishes.

L'OPERA LIRICA

....

THE LYRICAL WORK

WHEN FRIVOLOUS COURT AMUSEMENT BLOSSOMED INTO THE GREAT ITALIAN OPERATIC TRADITION of the 1800s, polite romantic innuendo gave way to a gamut of tragic emotions and dilemmas. Love, jealousy, lust, and bravery were beautifully expressed in the Italian language, with music and *grande sentimento*. The plots were filled with intrigue, and the inevitable climax of *opera lirica* was death—the tragedy that touches all. Orchestral crescendos and cries of desperate heroines, whether heard in a gilded opera house or driving to work, can bring even the coldest of hearts to tears—again and again.

GIUSEPPE VERDI 1813 - 1901	Revered as a man of the people; a quarter of a million attended his funeral. *Rigoletto, La Traviata, La Forza del Destino, Aida.*
GIACOMO PUCCINI 1858 - 1924	An ardent womanizer, he knew his subject intimately. *La Boheme, Tosca, Madama Butterfly, Turandot.*
CLAUDIO MONTEVERDI 1567 - 1643	The title role in his *Orfeo*, considered to be the first great Italian opera, was composed for a castrato.
GIOACCHINO ROSSINI 1792 - 1868	Best known for light opera; his *commedia dell'arte* masterpiece *Il Barbiere di Siviglia* was penned in thirteen days.
GAETANO DONIZETTI 1797 - 1848	Wrote over seventy operas, including *Lucia di Lammermoor*, before succumbing to syphilis. Exponent of *Bel Canto* style.

GLI ORFANI

FROM MEDIEVAL TIMES, THE IDEA OF CARRYING ON AN IMPORTANT FAMILY NAME AND, CONSEQUENTLY, FORtune, was of prime importance for an Italian. In order to insure the necessary male heir in a time of rampant child mortality, a woman had to bear as many children as possible. In a perpetual state of pregnancy, she would not be allowed to nurse her own children, but would instead engage the services of a *balia* (wet nurse). A desired position, this meant good nutrition, lodgings, and a stipend, but required the *balia* to abandon her own infant.

At the same time, to give inheritance and dowry precedence to the firstborn male and female in wealthy families, siblings were obligated by their families to enter religious orders, considered an honorable vocation. The close proximity of so many young and restless resulted in many unwanted births. What was to be done with all these foundlings? The first official orphanage in Europe opened in Florence in 1419. L'ospedale degli Innocenti, funded by the Silk Guild and several religious orders, offered a humane solution: children of all ages were clothed, fed, and trained in various trades. Today, the Florence phone book lists many *Innocenti* (the Innocent Ones), doubtless descendents of these *orfanelli*.

IL PARMIGIANO

. . . .

THE KING OF CHEESES

PARMIGIANO IS TRULY THE REIGNING MONARCH OF ITALIAN CHEESES—UNIVERSALLY BELOVED FOR ITS sweet, nutty flavor and distinctive golden color. It is a panacea for old and young alike, due to its high protein and mineral content, as well as digestibility (always an essential element in the constant gastronomic debate). So precious is Parmigiano that one of its varieties, Grana, is also a slang term for money.

It takes two gallons of milk to make one pound of Parmigiano. Each eighty-pound wheel is aged for two years in a painstaking hands-on process: numbered, brushed, polished, and tested throughout aging. All of the whey left over from the production is fed to an appreciative contingent of local pigs who will grow up to become prized Parma hams.

Parmigiano has more than its share of imitators; however, the European Court of Justice recently ruled that the cheese can be produced only in its legally designated area around Parma, where cows are fed exclusively local grass, hay, and natural vegetable feed. *Attenzione!* Parmigiano may not be used indiscriminately. Italians are as aghast at its use on seafood pasta as they are by a cappuccino ordered after a meal.

LA PASSEGGIATA

....

A S THE DAY COMES TO AN END, THE MAIN STREET IN VIRTUALLY EVERY ITALIAN TOWN OR VILLAGE SWELLS with activity as a large part of the local population naturally flocks together for the *passeggiata*, or evening stroll. People of all ages, meticulously dressed, intent on seeing and being seen, boisterously chatter while keeping a watchful eye on everything and everyone around them. Women friends arm in arm, young families with their perfect *bambini* in tow, groups of newly independent adolescents, and entwined *fidanzati* all promenade back and forth at a languid pace, while the older generations generally observe. If the church steps are too uncomfortable, some *nonni* will bring their own chairs, while men in fedoras congregate outside their favorite *caffè*, discussing politics in a haze of smoke.

On Saturdays in particular, this is the time to look in the shop windows, sip an *aperitivo*, greet friends and neighbors, coyly flirt, catch up on gossip, and make plans. The *passeggiata* has no prescribed destination, even though the main street typically ends in a piazza or church square. Then, like magic, the streets will suddenly empty, the shop shutters come down with a bang, and it's time for dinner. The *passeggiata* is over.

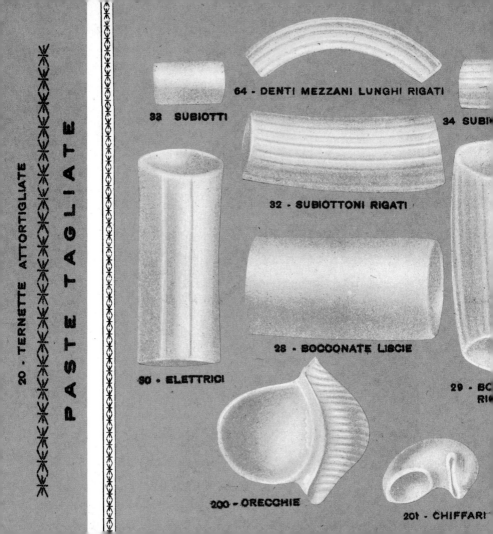

20 - TERNETTE ATTORTIGLIATE

PASTE TAGLIATE

64 - DENTI MEZZANI LUNGHI RIGATI

33 SUBIOTTI

34 SUBI

32 - SUBIOTTONI RIGATI

28 - BOCCONATE LISCIE

90 - ELETTRICI

29 - BC
RI

200 - ORECCHIE

201 - CHIFFARI

LA PASTA

....

ONCE EATEN OUT OF PAPER CONES SOLD BY STREET VENDORS, PASTA IS STILL TODAY A CONSTANT SOURCE of comfort, inspiration, and immense satisfaction. It knows no geographic or socioeconomic constraints: in Italy, everyone, north and south, rich and poor, loves pasta (except perhaps for Futurist F.T. Marinetti, who once called spaghetti "the absurd gastronomical religion of the Italians"). Historically, every region of Italy stakes a claim to its own distinctive design. Countless forms are illustrated in early pasta charts: *Pasta Tipo Genova,* from Genoa, typically spaghetti, depicted in voluptuous skeins; *Tipo Napoli,* or macaroni, from Naples, straight with a curve at the end where the strand had been hung out to dry; *tortellini,* conceived in Bologna to honor the navel of Venus; *pappardelle,* the wide noodles of Tuscany; *orecchiette* (little ears) from Puglia; and Sicilian *cannelloni.*

PASTA LORE

Il Museo Nazionale delle Paste Alimentari in Rome takes its subject seriously: working models of pasta-making machines, from the most ancient to high-tech; images of personalities as varied as Pulcinella and Sophia Loren, enjoying their favorite *primo piatto*; and most importantly, documentation to prove irrefutably that the precious noodle was in existence in twelfth-century Sicily, long before Marco Polo was credited with bringing it to Italy. www.museodellapasta.it

I PATRONI

....

BUON ONOMASTICO! EVERY DAY OF THE YEAR HAS AT LEAST ONE SAINT ASCRIBED TO IT, AND MOST ITALIAN calendars have these venerable souls listed prominently, along with the phases of the moon. The cards, the calls, the best wishes or small gifts given to celebrate one's *onomastico*, or name day, were once more commonplace than for an actual birthday. In addition, each town, large or small, has a patron saint, or protector, who must be duly honored on his or her respective day. The celebration includes a holiday for all of the shops and offices, a mass, a meal, and fireworks. The tradition is more heartfelt in the south where the festivities can be lavish, and statues of the saint are lovingly paraded through the town. However, in nineteenth-century Sicily, saints were blamed and their statues subsequently punished for "inadequate meteorological protection" when a severe drought crippled the island.

Recent popes have canonized numerous new saints, while inciting the wrath of many followers by revoking the sainthood of several revered subjects, such as Valentine, Ursula, and Christopher. Nonetheless, no truck driver in Italy would dream of getting behind the wheel without his San Cristoforo medallion.

Sᵃ DOROTHEA

SAN

Elisabetta Regi

NAME	DATE	SPECIALTY	INVOKED FOR
SAN BIAGIO	February 3	Wool workers and mattress makers	throat diseases
SANT'AGATA	February 5	Brass workers, nursing mothers, and bell ringers	volcanic eruptions and fires
SANT'APOLLONIA	February 9	Dentists	toothaches
SAN GIUSEPPE	March 19	Carpenters and fathers	to find work and to sell a house
SAN BERNARDINO di SIENA	May 20	Communicators and advertisers	lung disease and hoarseness
SANT'ANTONIO di PADOVA	June 13	Amputees, orphans, and shipwreck victims	missing objects and infertility
SANTA MARGHERITA	July 20	Laundresses, midwives, and expectant mothers	labor pains, bleeding, and storms
MARIA MADDALENA	July 22	Prostitutes and gardeners	fevers and penance
SAN CRISTOFORO*	July 25	Travelers and bachelors	safe travel

*sainthood revoked in 1969

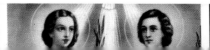

PREGHIERA A
ANTA APOLLONIA
VERGINE - MARTIRE

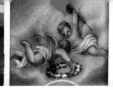

S. FRANCESCO

O glorioso nostro p...
cesco di Paola, che p...
ra operatore di tanti...
dalla gloria del Cie...
intercessione schiude...

NAME	DATE	SPECIALTY	INVOKED FOR
SANTA CHIARA	August 11	Clairvoyants, television, and laundry	good weather and communication
SANTA MONICA	August 27	Housewives, alcoholics, and disappointing children	trouble-free births
SANTA CATERINA di GENOVA	September 15	Difficult marriages and widows	temptation
SAN NICOLA di TOLENTINO	September 10	Injustice	converting sinners
S.S. COSIMO and DAMIANO	September 26	Barbers, druggists, and surgeons	bladder disease and gangrene
SAN FRANCESCO d'ASSISI	October 4	Animals and textile workers	poverty
SANTA CECILIA	November 22	Musicians and musical instrument makers	deafness
SANTA CATERINA d'ALESSANDRIA	November 25	Wheels and related professions (potters, spinners, knife grinders, and cyclists)	headaches and nursing mothers
SANTA LUCIA	December 13	Blind people, ophthalmologists, and electricians	blindness and eye problems
SANTO STEFANO	December 26	Bricklayers and stonemasons	kidney stones

LA PIAZZA

THE PIAZZA IS AN EXTENDED LIVING ROOM, ALWAYS OPEN TO ALL. FROM ANCIENT TIMES TO THE PRESENT day, it is the locus of all cultural and political energy of the city. As Italians did not often extend invitations to their homes, public and social life was conducted in the piazza. Official ceremonies, rebellions, tournaments, edicts, weddings, and all types of buying and selling took place in the open, where all could witness and participate. (To this day, Italians feel free to comment out loud—even to no one in particular—on whatever is happening around them.) The piazza knows no boundaries of gender, age, or class. Regardless of size or location, it is essential to the community. Where else can one read a newspaper, have a coffee, meet a friend, attend a political rally, listen to a concert, or observe the world in general?

PIAZZA	CITY	DISTINGUISHING CHARACTERISTICS
PIAZZA SAN MARCO	Venice	most pigeons and overpriced caffès
PIAZZA NAVONA	Rome	best baroque fountains and off-duty priests
PIAZZA DEL CAMPO	Siena	best sloped seating and most fluttering flags
PIAZZA DUOMO	Siracusa	best *passeggiata* and most gleaming pavement
PIAZZA GRANDE	Arezzo	best antique market and Vasari arcade
PIAZZA MAGGIORE	Bologna	most students and medieval architecture

PINOCCHIO

....

C'ERA UNA VOLTA UN PEZZO DI LEGNO. SO BEGINS THE TALE OF PINOCCHIO, THE BELOVED PRODIGAL SON who made good. In Italy he is as visible as Mickey Mouse, who appears to use the same tailor. Created by Florentine Carlo Lorenzini, who took his pen name from his mother's home town of Collodi, the trials of this naughty wooden puppet originally appeared in installments in one of Italy's first children's magazines from 1881 to 1883, soon after the unification of Italy. Collected in one volume as the novel *Pinocchio* in 1883, the book became a runaway success for readers young and old alike and went on to be translated into over one hundred languages, surpassed only by the Bible and the Koran. Why such appeal? Like Dante, Collodi wrote in the everyday Tuscan dialect, telling a story of common people, using metaphors to illustrate the human condition. He depicted class struggles and commented on social injustice, contrasting rich and poor. All of us in some way have been loved by a Geppetto, deceived by a fox, warned by a cricket, and felt hopeless in the belly of a whale. Savor the original translation—a deep and dark masterpiece that is a far cry from the Disney confection.

At the quaintly old-fashioned Parco di Pinocchio in the Tuscan town of Collodi, stroll through a leafy labyrinth of whimsical mosaics, sculptures, tableaux and fountains, where various Italian artists interpret the story of the celebrated puppet. Have lunch in the Michelucci-designed restaurant, tour the baroque terraced gardens of the adjacent sixteenth-century Villa Garzoni, and visit the charming butterfly museum. Open daily. www.pinocchio.it

LA PIZZA

PIZZA HAS EVERYTHING GOING FOR IT: IT IS FRAGRANT, DELICIOUS, AFFORDABLE, FAST TO MAKE, AND EASY TO eat. The perfect pizza is found in Naples, where the best mozzarella is made, and the tomatoes are rich and sweet from the sun. The crust must be slightly chewy, not too thick, not too thin, from dough made and shaped by hand. The expressive singsong dialect of the Neapolitan *pizzaiolo*, combined with a deft touch and mastery of the wood-burning ovens, makes for pure gastronomic bliss. It is here that the connoisseur learns that fewer ingredients make for better pizza, and that the creative abominations offered in other parts of the world (pineapple with goat cheese or peppersalamicheesemushroomsonionzucchinitomato in a deep dish) only confuse the palate. In fact, *verace pizza napoletana*, true Neapolitan pizza, has been approved for international DOC recognition.

MARGHERITA

The Romans had a simple wheat foccacia called *"picea,"* which, with a bit of yeast, olive oil, and salt, continued to be the staple of the poor. When tomatoes arrived in the area in the 1600s, a legend was born. The original was the *marinara*, named for the hungry fishermen who would be greeted with a hot pizza upon their return ashore. In 1889 when Queen Margherita came for a royal visit, chef Raffaele Esposito prepared and dedicated to her majesty the exquisite *Pizza Margherita,* crafted from tomato, mozzarella, and fresh basil leaves, representing the colors of the new Italian flag.

LE SCARPE

· · · · · · · · · · · ·

WHEN FIRST INTRODUCED TO AN ITALIAN, EXPECT A FURTIVE DOWNWARD GLANCE—THE SUBTLE CHECK-out-the-shoes reflex. For a country shaped like an elegant boot, it is only natural that footwear be a national obsession.

Shoes have always had their place in Italian history as status indicators. In Roman times, red sandals signified the highest rank. Centuries later, the upper classes wore elegant shoes to show that they didn't engage in demeaning labor. Frivolous Venetian ladies of the sixteenth century swayed on stilt-like *chopines* in order to keep their silken hems above the muck of the streets—of course, servants' assistance was essential for balance. And prescient fairy tale heroine Cenerentola (Cinderella) found true happiness only after finding that perfect little glass slipper.

CRAFT BECOMES ART

The temple of the world's most beautiful shoes, the Museo Salvatore Ferragamo in Florence is irresistible. Technical and artistic genius is evident in the extraordinarily innovative shoes of this modern master—colors, materials, and shapes never before imagined. Cork, velvet, raffia, beads, brocade, copper, cellophane, and fish skin delighted the feet of Greta, Sophia, Audrey, Rita, Lauren, Ava, and many more. Don't miss Marilyn's red rhinestone stiletto heels from her role in *Let's Make Love*. Selections from Ferragamo's archive of 10,000 creations, as well as original sketches, prototypes, and custom wooden forms, are on exhibit in this elegant space in the Palazzo Spini Feroni, Piazza Santa Trinità 5R, Florence.

LO SCONTRINO

....

"ASPETTI! LO SCONTRINO!" THERE IS A REASON FOR THE URGENCY WITH WHICH A SHOPKEEPER CALLS AFTER the departing customer, while waving a tiny white receipt. A recent measure taken by the Italian government to stem the flow of undeclared income is a strict law requiring every shop to issue a fiscal receipt for all purchases. The lack of this small square of paper can translate into a hefty fine for the shopkeeper (for not issuing) as well as the shopper (for not asking). Much uproar, protest, and finger-pointing ensued, until even the fruit and vegetable sellers at the market were required to follow the letter of the law—even for the purchase of one lemon. At the height of the crackdown, newspapers reported the tale of a hairdresser and his elderly mother who were both stiffly fined when she was apprehended leaving the salon with perfectly coiffed hair and no receipt. His protest, "But she's my *mother!*" was to no avail. Nevertheless, *furbini* (cunning ones) will always find a creative way around the law. In some cities, shopkeepers will send an escort out of the store with the shopper and her receipt. Upon safely turning the corner, the escort reclaims the *scontrino* and brings it back to the store to be used again…and again…and again.

LE SUPERSTIZIONI

....

SUPERSTITIONS

{1}

Il cappello sul letto mai. If you put your hat on the bed it means you will not be walking out the door again.

{2}

Olio versato porta male. It is bad luck to break a bottle of olive oil.

{3}

Non regalare ombrelli e fazzoletti, perché portano lacrime. Umbrellas and handkerchiefs should not be given as gifts; they will bring rain or tears.

A STRING OF CORAL BEADS AROUND A NEWBORN'S PUDGY WRIST IS BELIEVED TO PROTECT HER FROM any misfortune. From cradle to grave, Italians spend considerable effort keeping the devil at a distance. In the south, *corne,* or devil's horns, in coral, plastic, and wood appear on key chains, dashboards, front doors, and necks in an attempt to avoid consequences of the *malocchio*, or the Evil Eye. The most immediate and oft-used protection—almost a natural reflex—is making the gesture of the *corna,* in which the index and pinky finger are pointed downward, allowing the evil to discharge harmlessly deep into the earth. Hearing ambulance sirens, seeing a hearse, or mentioning a potential illness all warrant this iconic signal. The Italian male, not wanting his courage questioned, will make the motion with hand buried in pocket, doubly effective if he's able to touch his precious *coglioni* at the same time.

SEVENTEEN

Seventeen is the unlucky number in Italy. Conversely, thirteen is lucky, except when seating guests at a table—given the outcome of the Last Supper. In Mario Monicelli's madcap 1960 comedy *Risate di Gioia* (known in English as *Joyful Laughter* or *The Passionate Thief*), a Cinecittà extra played by Anna Magnani has no date for New Year's Eve. She is hastily invited to join a group of revelers, who subsequently ditch her upon the realization that she will bring the head count to thirteen. After a few more plot twists, she is reinvited in order to avoid the ill-fated number.

1. Il cappello sul letto mai.

2. Olio versato porta male.

3. Non regalare ombrelli e fazzo-letti, perché portano lacrime.

4. I piedi delle nubili non vanno spazzati.

5. Le cose appuntite vanno pagate.

6. Soldi sul letto portano male.

I TITOLI ONORIFICI

....

TITLES AND HONORIFICS

THERE WAS A TIME WHEN A TITLE SIGNIFIED ONE'S ELEVATED, NOBLE RANK: *PRINCIPE, CONTE, DUCA,* and *Marchese* were indications of the amount of land under their jurisdiction. Although the unification of Italy brought changes for the privileged class, a penchant for formal speech and flowery titles as well as social demarcation has allowed honorifics to continue to thrive in Italian culture. Anyone with a college degree of any kind is called *Dottore* (as are medical doctors). Students in elementary school are taught by a *maestro,* in high school by a *professore,* and at the university by a *Dottor Professore. Ingeniere* (Engineer), *Notaio* (Notary), *Avvocato* (Attorney), *Architetto* (Architect), and *Geometra* (Surveyor) are all titles that appear on business cards, doorbells, and in morning greetings at the local *caffè: "Buon giorno, Architetto Rossi!"* As always, church and politics comprise categories of their own. High-ranking politicians are referred to as *Eccellenza,* or Your Excellency. (The victims of flagrant Mafia murders of important judges and politicians were referred to as "excellent cadavers.") A bishop or cardinal is an *Eminenza.* The Pope is *Sua Santità*—His Holiness. It doesn't get any better than that.

INGEGNERE

Lega

PAL
21

A. Rossini

ARCHITETTO

Dott. Ing. Alfonzo Agosti

Piazza Di S. Maria Novella, 16
50123 Firenze   Tel. 055

Gabriele DiSpiri

ARCHITETTO

VIA MELISURGO GUGL
80133 NAPOLI (NA),
081 7647589

VIA DA PALESTR
00193 ROMA (

S. MARCO, 5472
30124 VENEZIA (VE), ITALIA   GABRIEL

David Rus

ECONOMICA

Dott. Ing. Elisto Palumbo

VIA DEI GIUDICATI, 1
09131 CAGLIARI (SS), ITA
070 47490

VIA DEI SERVI, 9/R   055 2647467

LA VENDEMMIA

....

AS AUGUST COMES TO AN END AND THE DAYS GROW SHORTER, THERE IS A COOL TINGE TO THE NIGHT. The excitement is palpable as grape farmers and winemakers watch the sky and watch the vines; the sky, the vines. The perfect ripeness of the grapes is what is awaited—and this will vary with the weather. A balance of sun and rain is essential, and harvest time will fluctuate as much as twenty days from year to year. A severe summer drought or a rainstorm too late in the season can mean disaster for the crops. In difficult moments like these, the aid of Minerva, goddess of wisdom and protectress of winemaking, is often solicited. *La vendemmia* begins with the white grapes, which ripen before the red. All over Italy, vineyards are animated with brightly dressed pickers, and roads hum with slow-moving tractors piled high with glistening clusters of grapes heading to the cantinas. The rich perfume of earth, sun, and grape envelops the courtyard where the fruit is sorted, washed, stemmed, and crushed in a flurry of activity, as the older generation passes on the artful process of winemaking. Crisp autumn weather and hearty communal meals make the *vendemmia* an anticipated event, with the entire extended family on hand to help.

LA VESPA

. . . .

THE MOTOR SCOOTER

"*COM'È BELLO ANDARE IN VESPA, CON I PIEDI SOPRA LA TESTA...*" (HOW LOVELY TO BE ON A VESPA, WITH your feet over your head…) So goes the popular tune celebrating the practical but sexy scooter that changed the face of a nation. Post World War II Italy was in dire need of inexpensive and practical transportation, and the Piaggio family, looking for a new direction after their fighter plane facility was bombed, promptly answered the call.

"*Sembra una vespa!*" (It looks like a wasp!) declared Enrico Piaggio upon seeing the prototype in 1946, and an international design icon was born. With its elegant lines and ability to be parked virtually anywhere, the Vespa is quintessentially Italian, and nowhere in Italy is one spared its familiar high-octave buzzing. The vehicle of choice for businessmen, nuns, teenagers, and grandmothers alike, the Vespa features a removable protective front shield that keeps even the impeccably dressed mud-free.

Sales skyrocketed in 1953 when Audrey Hepburn joined Gregory Peck for a spin on his Vespa in *Roman Holiday*. Although recent laws require a license (available at age fourteen) and helmet, the Vespa continues to provide a rite of passage and the wings of youth.

The Ape (pronounced Ah-pay), or "bee," the three-wheeled Vespa sibling, is the miniature Italian pickup truck. Performing seemingly Herculean feats, the Ape is used to transport everything from vegetables to plate glass windows. They are seen (and heard) everywhere, navigating medieval city streets as well as hilly country roads, carrying entire families, roomsful of mismatched furniture, or crates of newly hatched chicks en route to market.

BIBLIOGRAPHY

Agnesi, Eva. *L'Ora della Pasta*. Rome: Museo Nationale delle Paste Alimentari, 1998.

Barzini, Luigi. *The Italians*. New York: Atheneum, 1964.

Bondanella, Peter. *Italian Cinema: From Neorealism to the Present*. New York: Continuum, 1983.

Calamari, Barbara and DiPasqua, Sandra. *Patron Saints*. New York: Abrams, 2007.

De Jorio, Andrea. *Gesture in Naples and Gesture in Classical Antiquity*. Bloomington: Indiana University Press, 2000.

Falasca-Zamponi, Simonetta. *Fascist Spectacle: The Aesthetics of Power in Mussolini's Italy*. Berkeley: University of California Press, 2000.

Field, Carol. *Celebrating Italy*. New York: William Morrow and Company, 1990.

Hofmann, Paul. *That Fine Italian Hand*. New York: Henry Holt, 1991.

ABOUT the AUTHORS

Louise Fili is principal of Louise Fili Ltd, a New York City graphic design firm specializing in logos, food packaging, and restaurant identities. She has co-authored, with Steven Heller, over a dozen books on design, including *Euro Deco* and *Stylepedia*. She also wrote and designed *The Civilized Shopper's Guide to Florence* for The Little Bookroom. In 2004 she was inducted into the Art Directors Hall of Fame.

Lise Apatoff was born and raised in Chicago and moved to Italy in 1978 after receiving her Master of Fine Arts degree. She lives on a farm in the Tuscan countryside north of Florence with her Italian husband and their son. Using her intimate knowledge of art, history, and Italian culture, she works extensively as a museum lecturer, teacher, and travel guide throughout Italy.